IMAGES OF LONDON

ELTHAM

IMAGES OF LONDON

ELTHAM

DAVID SLEEP

TEMPUS

Fontispiece: Eltham and Mottingham Cottage Hospital. The hospital was located in the lower part of the High Street near St John's church. It was established in 1880 and served the local community until 1898 when a new hospital was built in Park Place, now known as Passey Place. The old hospital building was bought by Mr W. Hitches and incorporated into his new cycle and motor business. Today this is the site of the new Nissan car showrooms, which opened in 2004.

First published 2004

Tempus Publishing Limited
The Mill, Brimscombe Port,
Stroud, Gloucestershire, GL5 2QG
www.tempus-publishing.com

© David Sleep 2004

The right of David Sleep to be identified as the Author
of this work has been asserted in accordance with the
Copyrights, Designs and Patents Act 1988.

British Library Cataloguing in Publication Data.
A catalogue record for this book is available from the British Library.

ISBN 0 7524 3381 4
Typesetting and origination by Tempus Publishing Limited.
Printed in Great Britain.

Contents

Acknowledgements

The majority of pictures used in this book are from my own collection of picture postcards, photographs and antiquarian prints. However, I greatly acknowledge the loan from the Eltham Society's photographic collection; several of the pictures used in this publication and those acquired from the collections of Gus White.

I also greatly appreciate members of the Eltham Society publications committee, John Kennett, John Towey and Gus White, for all their support and encouragement. I wish to pay particular thanks to John Kennett who has been an inspiration to me over many years particularly when pursuing my interest in Eltham's history; I thank him also for reading through the text and making useful suggestions.

Introduction

Eltham is first recorded in the Domesday Book of 1086, although the name Eltham can trace its origins back to Saxon times, meaning 'Elta's Homestead', 'Home of the Swans' or 'Old Home'. Whilst no evidence exists of occupation before these records, it is most likely that there was a settlement in Saxon times. There are even earlier records of the existence of Mottingham from a ninth-century charter, which shows occupation of the area to date from 862 AD.

The Domesday Book records that the manor of Eltham was then in the possession of Odo, Bishop of Bayeux, and the Earl of Kent and held for him by Haimo, the Sheriff of the county. Odo was a half-brother of William the Conqueror who had been given land in Kent following the Norman conquest of England. The manor consisted of 1½ sulongs (a measure of arable land); land for twelve ploughs, forty-two villagers with twelve small holders, nine slaves; meadow of 22 acres and woodland with fifty pigs. The population was around 270 people. The first church in Eltham stood beside the present day St John the Baptist parish church in the High Street at the corner of Well Hall Road and its first priest was Adam de Bromleigh in 1160.

The manor had a number of owners before being passed to Anthony Bek, the Bishop of Durham, in 1295. Bek began work on his residence where Eltham Palace now stands and in 1305 he presented the manor to the Prince of Wales, the future Edward II. It is at this point that the long association for Eltham with the medieval and Tudor monarchs begins. Prince John, the second son of Edward II and Queen Isabella was born at Eltham in 1316 and was baptized in the manor's royal chapel.

Farming around the Eltham area developed throughout the middle ages and royal deer parks called Great, Middle and Horne were created around Eltham Palace. Housing developed along Eltham High Street and by the middle of the thirteenth century an estate and manor were created at Well Hall, its first owner being Matthew De Hegham in 1253. Another notable owner was Sir John Pulteney who was Lord Mayor of London four times in the 1330s.

In the 1470s Eltham Palace saw some of its most ambitious work with the building of the present great hall during the reign of Edward IV. The great hall, with its fine hammer-beam roof devised originally for Westminster Hall, was completed by 1482. A new range of royal apartments was built during Henry VII's reign and his second son, the future Henry VIII, spent much of his boyhood at Eltham and built a new chapel during his reign. In 1525 regulations for the royal household were drawn up by Cardinal Thomas Wolsey while he was staying at Eltham Palace and these became known as The Statutes of Eltham. Henry VIII's reign marked the beginning of the end for Eltham as a royal residence, as Greenwich came into favour for its closeness to the river and easier access to London.

Almshouses for needy people were built in Eltham, the earliest being the Thomas Philipot almshouses, which were built in 1694 on the High Street near the corner with Blunts Road. The row of six houses survived until 1929 when they were demolished for road widening and replacement housing was built in Philipot Path. More wealthy people also came to Eltham and built large houses with extensive rear gardens along the High Street. One of the houses that still survives in the High Street today is Cliefden House, built in about 1720 and located opposite Passey Place (formerly Park Place).

With the coming of the railway, the population of Eltham steadily increased from under 2,000 in 1801 to just over 2,500 in 1851 and nearly 6,000 in 1881. The first railway station was Eltham (now Mottingham), which opened on the 1 September 1866 on the Lewisham to Dartford via Sidcup loop line. The station was located one mile south of the High Street, but this helped in the development of Mottingham with new houses and shops around what is known today as Mottingham village along Mottingham Road. With the opening of Pope Street (now New Eltham) station in 1878 this allowed New Eltham to expand from its rural setting and scattering of cottages.

On 1 May 1895 the Bexleyheath railway line opened, running from Blackheath to Dartford. Eltham residents were served by Well Hall station and then by another station called Shooters Hill and Eltham Park, which opened in 1908 to serve the residents of the newly built Corbett housing estate. The station name was shortened to just Eltham Park in 1927. In 1985 Eltham Well Hall station as it had become known, was closed together with Eltham Park due to the construction of the Rochester Way relief road and a new station named Eltham was built just east of the old Eltham (Well Hall) station across Well Hall Road.

The Eltham area is unique in its wide expanse of open spaces and woodland. From the ancient woodlands of Oxleas Wood on the south side of Shooters Hill to the public and recreational parks around Eltham Park and Avery Hill, there is much to offer residents and visitors to the area. In part this has been helped by Eltham's long association with the Crown and local campaigns to save large areas of open ground.

Housing in Eltham continued at great pace in the early twentieth century. In 1900 the construction of the grid-pattern design of the Corbett Estate in Eltham Park and Well Hall started. With the coming of the First World War there was a need to house a great number of munitions workers at Woolwich Arsenal. In early 1915 work began on the Well Hall Estate (now Progress Estate) and by the end of the year nearly 1,300 houses and flats were completed. Additional housing for the workers was constructed in the form of temporary hutments on land designated for the Corbett Estate. New housing continued at a pace in the early 1930s at Middle Park, Horn Park, New Eltham and Mottingham.

The Eltham area has its fair share of famous people and writers who were either born in Eltham or resided there for part of their life. Bob Hope the famous comedian was born at 44 Craigton Road, part of the Corbett Estate on 29 May 1903. The comedian and star of many films Frankie Howerd lived in one of the temporary wooden hutments in Arbroath Road and attended Gordon School. The politician Denis Healey (now Lord Healey of Riddlesden) was born in Grove Park Road in Mottingham, opposite Eltham College, in 1917 and also lived in one of the temporary hutments for munitions workers at Rosyth Road. The famous cricketer W.G. Grace lived at Fairmount (now a residential home) in Mottingham Lane from 1909 until his death 1915. A blue plaque was unveiled in 1966 at Fairmount to commemorate his residence there. Another blue plaque in Archery Road commemorates the residence of one time Home Secretary and Deputy Prime Minister, Herbert Morrison, who also lived at two other houses in Eltham. He died in 1965.

In this book I have attempted to capture the Eltham area from as early as the first-quarter of the twentieth century through a variety of picture postcards and photographs, antiquarian prints and recent photographs. This book illustrates Eltham's rich and absorbing history and its development from a village into a busy and active suburban town and district. Pictures have been used to include the whole of the SE9 postal district, one of the largest postal districts in London, which includes parts of Mottingham, which itself is divided between the London boroughs of Greenwich and Bromley. Eltham continues to be a developing area, but still retains its strong connections with the past and the monarchy. In 1970 Her Majesty Queen Elizabeth II visited Eltham Palace to mark the fiftieth anniversary of the Royal Army Educational Corps, and as recently as July 2004 the Prince of Wales made a private visit to Eltham Palace. In recent times we have seen the restoration of the Courtauld wing at Eltham Palace and gardens to bring them back to their 1930s' splendour; the restoration of Well Hall Pleasaunce to once again capture that municipal pride; the restoration of The Orangery to bring a much neglected building to stand proud and show its eighteenth century features and the campaign to preserve Severndroog Castle as a place to be enjoyed.

I hope you will enjoy looking through this book and being reminded of bygone days, whilst still remembering that the Eltham area is a changing and developing place. I hope that it will encourage you to go out and explore its mixture of open green spaces, historic sites and all the amenities it has to offer.

David Sleep
July, 2004

one

Eltham
High Street

Eltham parish church of St John the baptist was designed by Sir Arthur Blomfield. It is seen here in around 1913 with Court Yard to the left amd Well Hall Road to the right. Note a No. 39 bus on route to Sidcup. This bus route ran through Eltham between 1912 and 1914.

A Victorian view of St John's church before it was rebuilt in 1875.

Another Victorian view of the old church of St John. This church can be dated back to the twelfth century when, in 1160, it was recorded that the first rector was Adam de Bromleigh.

St John's church from Court Yard. The new church with the rebuilt tower and spire was completed in 1879. Note the drinking water fountain of 1886, which is still in position there today.

A view of the church from the High Street in around 1907. The lychgate was built in 1881 as a memorial to a former churchwarden, Richard Mills. The public conveniences did not come until 1912. Note the Borough of Woolwich horse and cart.

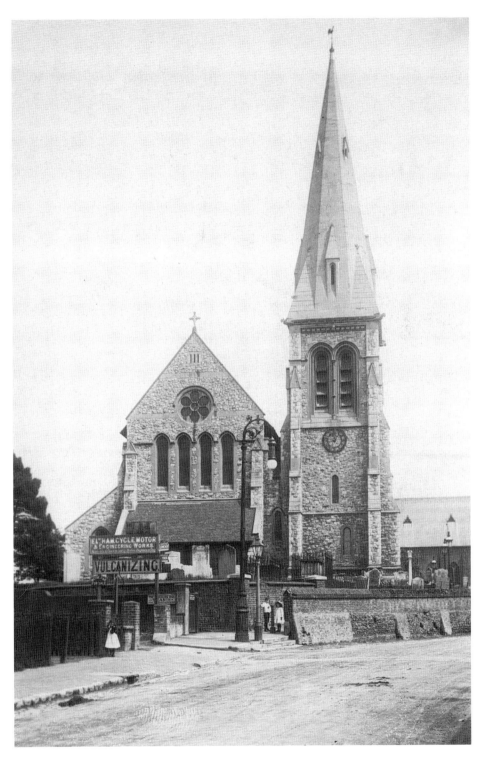

The church looking towards the crossroads with Eltham Cycle Motor and Engineering Works on the left. Note the railings around the tombs.

INTERIOR, THE PARISH CHURCH, ELTHAM. 128.

This interior view of St John's church from around 1920 shows the nave looking towards a wrought-iron screen in the chancel arch. Much of this area was altered in 1983.

On the brick wall is the 1924 Eltham war memorial cross. It shows the memorial before the names of those who died in the First World War were inscribed on it. Wreaths are still laid here each year on Remembrance Sunday.

Above & below: These old bells were removed from St John's church in 1924 and were recast by Gillett & Johnson's bell foundry at Croydon. Note the parish beadle to the left on the first picture and again pictured in the second.

Looking up the High Street in 1906 with the Eltham Dairy, The Greyhound public house and Mellins the chemist on the right. The earliest mention of Mellins dates back to 1870. The chemist finally closed in 1972 and is currently used as a restaurant.

A similar view from 1935. It shows the High Street much busier, with overhead cables for the trams that were introduced in 1910 and terminated at Eltham church. The building in the middle of the photograph was the domed roof for the Palace cinema, built in 1922 and demolished in 1972.

The Greyhound public house in 1905. The building can date its origins back to the 1720s. Note the pub sign with the licensee name H. Elms. The Elms family came to Eltham in 1897 and was associated with The Greyhound until 1970.

A later view of The Greyhound public house, which has undergone a number of alterations over the years. It is now a Grade II listed building.

A view of Park Place (renamed Passey Place in 1938) in 1909 looking towards North Park from the High Street.

A similar view showing the Eltham post office that opened in 1912 and was extended in 1935. The building closed in 1972 and the post office was relocated to its present site in Court Yard. The building is now used as a public house called the Old Post Office, which opened in 1995.

Eltham and Mottingham Cottage Hospital in Park Place in around 1919. The hospital was opened in 1898 and served the local community until its closure in March 1980.

Houses on the north side of North Park in around 1907. North Park ran parallel with the High Street. It was not until the 1920s that there was a direct route through North Park, between Court Road and Footscray Road. This is now the site of flats called woodington Close.

The premises of David Greig, the grocery and provision merchant, was built in 1905 and remained open until 1974. The Edwardian upper part of the building can still be seen today above the Iceland store. Note the unusual three-wheeled delivery vehicle advertising pure lard at 6½ d.

Looking up the High Street in around 1907. The Castle Hotel public house on the right was built at the turn of the twentieth century replacing an earlier hostelry. It offered accommodation to visitors and was the scene of many dinners and functions of local organisations. The site was redeveloped in 1961.

Looking down the narrow High Street in around 1907. The Castle Hotel is on the left (now the site of Superdrug and KFC). Further down is the David Greig building.

Eltham's horse bus service in around 1905. The official bus stop was outside The Castle Hotel. This Tillings service ran from Eltham to Blackheath via Lee Green and was withdrawn in 1908.

Ram Alley in around 1905. This old cottage became the site of the recently closed Alders department store, which has since undergone renovation and is part of a new development of shops, including Peacocks, MFI and JJB Sports.

Right: Another view of Ram Alley in around 1905, looking towards the High Street.

Below: W. Metcalfe in around 1904. In 2002, J. Metcalfe & Son (Eltham) Ltd celebrated 200 years as a family business in Eltham. It began in 1802 as a smithy and forge and the family continued shoeing horses until 1959. The photograph shows the premises in the High Street (now the site of Woolworth's). The family now specialises in the repair and sales of lawn-mowers, and are located in Passey Place.

Above: Tucked away behind the High Street in Orangery Lane is a fine piece of garden architecture called The Orangery. The building was associated with Eltham House, which stood on the High Street and was demolished in 1937 for shop development (now Debenhams). The building dates back to 1723 and has miraculously survived for nearly 300 years.

Left: A closer view above the doorway. In this semi-circular round-headed niche would have stood a carved stone eagle. Both these photographs were taken in the early 1980s before major restoration was completed in 2003 and has brought this most neglected building back to life again.

Eltham's public library in 1912. The library opened in 1906 and was part of an ambitious scheme of municipal buildings to include a town hall and swimming baths. The library was the only part of the plan that was built and this Grade II listed building today remains as an impressive feature of the Edwardian era.

An open top No.21 bus outside Eltham library. The route No.21 bus service started in 1908 and originally ran from Oxford Street to Sidcup. The service through Eltham was replaced in 1997 with the No.321 bus route from New Cross to Sidcup.

Above: The library is on the left with The Rising Sun public house in the centre of the photograph in around 1915. The Philipot almshouses are in the distance.

Left: The Rising Sun public house in around 1905. The original Rising Sun was demolished to make way for the proposed municipal buildings scheme. The present building opened its doors in 1904.

Opposite: A gentleman's charabanc outing on a Timpson's coach outside The Rising Sun public house, probably in the 1920s.

The Philipot almshouses in around 1910. The almshouses extended to Blunts Road. This fine row of houses was originally built in 1694 and finally had to be demolished in 1931 for road widening. Replacement almshouses were built on land off Passey Place and the original date stone was set into the brickwork.

This row of cottages in Pound Place dated back to the seventeenth century and were demolished in the late 1920s. The shop on the corner was a sweet shop. The photograph is from 1906. The corner of Pound Place and the High Street is now occupied by the Lunn Poly travel agents.

Christ Church priory from the garden. The house to the left, known as Eagle House, was acquired by the Catholic Church in 1910 and renamed Christ Church priory. The picture shows the church before extensions in 1936.

The interior of Christ Church when it was originally built.

The centre of the picture shows the former Eltham workhouse of 1738, which later was converted to almshouses and demolished in 1964. The site is located opposite the fire station and was replaced by shops.

Outside Eltham little cinema at the end of the First World War. This was Eltham's first motion picture house built in 1913 and showed films up to the early 1930s. The building was demolished in 1968. The site is now occupied by a new housing development promoted as Royal Eltham Heights on the corner of the High Street and Westmount Road.

This building was Eltham's police station between 1865 and 1939. It stood on the corner of Footscray Road (formerly Victoria Road) and the High Street. Note the plaque on the side of the building showing Victoria Road leading to Footscray and Maidstone. The site is now occupied by the Blockbuster store.

Eltham's fire station in around 1907. The photograph also shows part of the building on the left used as Eltham's police station. Beyond the four shops is the fire station opened in 1904. The Man of Kent public house is to the right of the fire station. Most of the space to the front of these buildings was lost to road widening in 1933.

Court Yard in 1902. The Crown public house is on the left before the row of cottages. The original Crown public house was built in 1810 and rebuilt in 1930. The present day post office occupies the site at the end of the cottages. The large elm tree seen by the cottages was blown down during a storm in 1903.

Court Yard, looking back towards the crossroads of the High Street, in around 1913. A row of cottages can be seen on the right. Grummitt's hardware store is now occupied by Robinson, Szabo & Jackson estate agents. Shops to the left were replaced by Grove Market Place, the first opening as a Wimpy in May 1967. A tram can be seen in the distance.

A view of Court Yard in around 1903 with Wythfield Road (then Wellington Road) on the left and Philipot Path (then Back Lane) leading to Park Place on the right. The Eltham congregational church spire can be seen in the distance.

The Eltham congregational church with Sherard House on the right. Sherard House dates back to 1634; it was demolished to make way for the National Westminster Bank, which opened in 1922. The house to the left was demolished in 1905 for the construction of Well Hall Road linking the High Street with Well Hall station. The church was demolished in 1936 due to the increase in traffic and tram noise and a new church was built in Court Road, now called the Eltham United Reformed church.

The Eltham Congregational church was consecrated in 1868 and stood on the corner of the High Street and Well Hall Road. The site is now occupied by McDonalds; the basement of the church still survives and would have been used as the Sunday school hall.

The Kings Arms public house in around 1915, opposite Eltham's parish church. A section of the church wall can be seen on the left. The public house, together with the buildings shown, was demolished in the 1920s to make way for road widening and the tram route extension.

The lower part of the High Street in around 1934. On the right is The Chequers public house, rebuilt in 1904 and now a café and cocktail bar. A milestone standing outside the public house marks eight miles to London Bridge and four miles to Footscray. Note the Hitche's garage sign, which was the original site of Eltham and Mottingham cottage hospital until 1898 when it moved to Park Place. The Nissan showrooms now occupy the site. Beyond St John's church is the spire of the Eltham Congregational church, which was demolished a few years after this picture was taken.

The White Hart public house in around 1905. The public house at No.2 Eltham High Street was rebuilt in 1926. Note the horse-drawn cart making a stop outside the public house. A grocery shop to the left sold Liptons tea, R. White's ginger beer, teas and sandwiches.

The newly rebuilt White Hart public house in 1927 on the right. It is still in use as a public house today.

An aerial view showing Eltham Hill School and part of the Woolwich Borough Council Page Estate to the left. The school was built in 1927 and the view shows the school long before it was enlarged in the 1970s. A date for this view is likely to be 1927 as it does not show the building of the Eltham Hill club, which opened in 1928. In the school grounds stands an eighteenth century summerhouse, known locally as the Van Dyck Pavilion, possibly due to the painter's association with nearby Eltham Palace where he was given apartments during the reign of Charles I.

Above: In an area called Middle Park to the south of Eltham Hill, once part of the royal enclosures surrounding Eltham Palace, is a large area of housing built from the early 1930s. With the construction of housing there was a need for a church. The construction of St Saviour's church in Middle Park Avenue began in 1932, was completed in less than eight months and was intended to seat some 500 worshippers.

Left: St Saviour's church in Middle Park. The interior of the church looking at the nave towards the sanctuary at the east end. The pulpit is on the right.

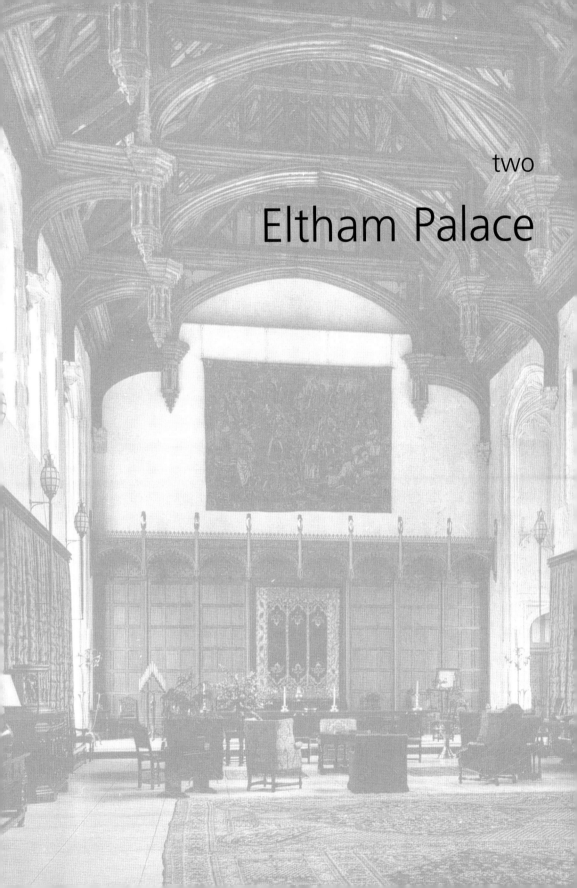

two

Eltham Palace

King John's Palace in 1792. An antiquarian print of the great hall at Eltham Palace drawn in 1792 and seen from the north. The great hall at this time was used as a barn and many artists, notably J.M.W. Turner and Paul Sandby, came to Eltham to draw and paint this romantic ruin. Eltham had been a royal home to the medieval and Tudor kings and queens of England from 1305 when the then owner of the Manor of Eltham, Anthony Bek the Bishop of Durham, presented it to Edward Prince of Wales, the future Edward II. The name King John's Palace, which appears on many of the early prints and photographic postcards, probably arose from either the association with Prince John, the second son of Edward II and his queen Isabella, who was born at Eltham in 1316 and is still known today as Prince John of Eltham or King John II of France who, after the French defeat at the battle of Poitiers in 1356, was brought to England and held for a time at the palace as Edward III's prisoner.

Tomb of John of Eltham,
Eltham Palace.

KENT.

An antiquarian print of the tomb of Prince John of Eltham in Westminster Abbey. In 1336, while campaigning in Scotland for his elder brother Edward III, Prince John contracted a fever and died at Perth at the early age of twenty. Edward III escorted his brother's body back to London and his funeral took place in Westminster Abbey on 15 January 1337. The tomb originally had a canopy above the monument but this collapsed in 1776. Each year the Eltham Society sponsors an event as part of the society's schools local history project where six children and their teacher from an Eltham primary school attend Eltham Palace to collect flowers from the gardens and then take them to Westminster Abbey to be laid on Prince John's tomb as a commemoration to the Prince's connection with Eltham.

Eltham Palace from the north-east in 1735. Eltham had been the boyhood home of Henry VIII, however, after the English Civil War much of the palace fell into decay and only the great hall, built in 1479 during the reign of Edward IV, substantially remains. The moat bridge in the foreground can trace its origins back to the reign of Richard II in the late fourteenth century.

The great hall from the south is shown in a ruinous state with a number of farm buildings surrounding it. This antiquarian print was made into a postcard and produced in the Edwardian period.

This view from the east and across the moat was taken in around 1911. It shows a building known as Moat House to the right, and the dwellings called Eltham Court, occupied by the tenant Mr Richard Bloxham in the Victorian era, to the left. The great hall is in the background.

A closer view of Eltham Court in around 1911 from the north side showing the north door to the great hall. Note that there is no glass in the windows. The section adjoining the great hall was built during Mr Bloxham's tenancy and is dated 1859 as shown by the date sign above the first floor window. The gables incorporated into the house, shown on the left, formed part of the old palace and in parts date back to Tudor times.

The great hall from the north in around 1906. Visitors could visit the great hall through the gate to the left of the lodge building after receiving permission from the tenant of Eltham Court. The date sign of 1859 (as seen in the previous picture) on Eltham Court is on the extreme left.

A view of the great hall and Eltham Court from across the south dry moat in the 1920s. Traces of the south moat bridge are on the left.

The great hall and Eltham Court from the south side from a photograph taken around 1905. The lawn in front of the great hall and house was the site of kitchens and several inner courtyards from the medieval and Tudor palace, none of which have yet been excavated.

The great hall around 1905. Note the ruinous state of the great hall with no glass in the window frames. It was not until 1911 that major works were carried out by the Office of Works.

Interior of the great hall in around 1905 looking east towards a timber structure possibly showing remnants of the medieval screen passage. The hall is dominated by the fine hammer-beam roof constructed in the 1470s. During the major works of 1911, the roof was strengthened with the insertion of steel braces. As can be seen, at this time the great hall was being used as a tennis court.

Above: Looking towards the great hall from the Edwardian gardens. Parts of the wall surrounding the great hall and inner courtyard of the palace can be dated back to the time of Anthony Bek. In this view the wall is almost covered with the growth of the gardens. Today this area is the sunken rose garden.

Right: An Edwardian gardener in around 1906 stands in the dry moat at the entrance to a Tudor refuse tunnel, which discharged into the moat.

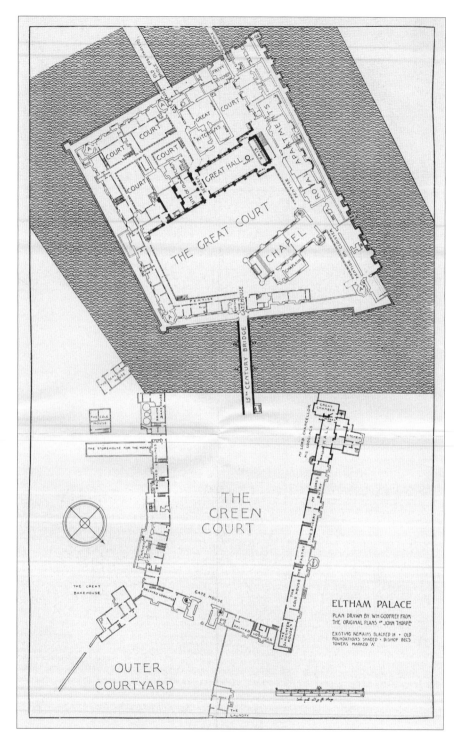

A plan of Eltham Palace based on an original from 1590 shows the palace at the height of its fame. The great hall, foundations of royal apartments, moat bridge and walls are all that remains today of this once favourite royal home of the English monarchs.

A late 1930s aerial view showing parts of the newly designed gardens and between the great hall and the moat bridge the v-shaped design of Eltham Hall. The hall was the residence of Stephen and Virginia Courtauld from 1936 to 1944. The tenancy to Eltham Court expired in 1933 and the Courtaulds were given permission to demolish it so long as they retained the Tudor gables and restored the great hall. This photograph was taken before excavations of the royal apartments, which extended right of the great hall along the moat wall, were conducted in the early 1950s.

A view of Eltham Hall from the rock garden shortly after completion of the house in 1935. The loggia, which led into the entrance hall from the garden side, was decorated with four reliefs carved by Gilbert Ledward. The reliefs depicted the interests of Stephen and Virginia Courtauld, including yachting and mountaineering.

A view of the entrance to Eltham Hall and the north side of the great hall from the late 1930s. Part of the Tudor gables incorporated into the new house can be seen on the left. Over the main entrance to the house was a sculpture dedicated to Hospitality by Carleton Attwood of Swindon, which is a most welcoming sign on entering the house into the domed ceiling of the entrance hall.

A 1930s view from across the south moat showing the restored great hall and adjoining Eltham Hall. Stephen and Virginia Courtauld used the great hall as one of their main reception rooms and built an extension to the left, which included an orangery and squash court.

The interior of the great hall as furnished for Stephen and Virginia Courtauld in 1937. This photograph was taken from beneath the minstrels gallery looking across the stone floor towards the dais at the far end of the hall, which was a timber screen designed and constructed by the architects of the house, John Seely and Paul Paget, based on a fifteenth-century rood screen from St Mary's church, Attleborough in Norfolk. The Courtaulds left Eltham in 1944 and the house became home of the Royal Army Educational Corps. In the late 1990s English Heritage undertook a major restoration programme, which has returned the house and great hall to its appearance in the 1930s and '40s. It has been described as the finest art deco interior in England.

A later photograph of the great hall when occupied by the Royal Army Educational Corps from 1945 to 1992. It shows the wooden flooring installed by the corps and without the lanterns shown in the previous photograph. The replica banners are of the Knights of the Garter, which, it is reputedly said, was established at Eltham in 1347 during the reign of Edward III.

Following the opening of the restored house and great hall in 1999, English Heritage undertook a major scheme to recreate the gardens to resemble their 1930s appearance. The south moat border seen here was part of their contemporary gardens scheme. English Heritage was presented with an Eltham Society award in 2001 for the remarkable restoration of the gardens.

Looking across the moat from the bridge towards the Moat House around 1905. The house became a private hotel in 1921 but, along with Eltham Court, was demolished to make way for the new Eltham Hall in 1933.

The Moat House, moat and bridge seen from the east in 1912 from what is now the site of the rock garden.

Looking across the moat bridge towards the Lord Chancellor's lodgings in around 1912. The buildings can in part be dated back to the sixteenth century and, notably, were occupied by Cardinal Thomas Wolsey, Lord Chancellor to Henry VIII and Sir Christopher Hatton, Lord Chancellor to Elizabeth I. The buildings still survive today, although they have been upgraded and are now very desirable properties.

A view of the Lord Chancellor's lodgings from Court Yard in aound 1906 with a lane to the left known at the time as Bridle Lane and now today as King John's Walk.

The Gatehouse in around 1916. This large house is in Court Yard at the corner with Tilt Yard Approach. The house replaced an earlier property called Court Yard House. It was built in 1913 for the writer Ellen Thorneycroft Fowler and her husband Alfred Felkin. The house is located close to the site of the original gatehouse to the palace in the area known as the green court (see the earlier 1590 plan on p. 48).

A garden fête and bazaar was held at Eltham Palace on the 13 and 14 June 1924 called Ye Olde Eltham Fayre. Some of the people participating in the event in Tudor costumes stand by the moat bridge.

Above: A group of ladies at the Ye Olde Eltham Fayre in their fine costumes stand by the south door of the great hall.

Right: The front cover of the programme for the Ye Old Eltham Fayre.

A view of Eltham Lodge in around 1908 to the east of the palace in an area which was known in medieval times as the Great Park. Sir John Shaw, a financial supporter to Charles II, was granted a lease to the estate in 1663 and built himself a house away from the palace buildings, which had by now become ruinous. The Shaw family remained at Eltham Lodge until 1820.

Eltham Lodge in 1904. In 1892 the Crown lease of the estate and Eltham Lodge was transferred to the Eltham Golf Club. In 1923 the club amalgamated with the Royal Blackheath Golf Club, which still retains the site today and uses the building as the clubhouse.

three

Well Hall

Well Hall Road in 1912 looking towards Well Hall station. The row of houses on the left known as Spencer Gardens were built in 1906. Lassa Road to the left separates these houses. Note the tram lines.

This view of Well Hall Road from Lassa Road shows the hostels for munitions workers from Woolwich Arsenal. Note the bread-cart belonging to J.B. Fyson, whose bakery was at No.94 Eltham High Street, with a delivery basket from a well-known name, Hovis.

Above & below: Exterior and interior views of the dining room of the girls' hostels in Well Hall Road in around 1918. Temporary hostels and hutments were constructed during the First World War to assist with accommodation for the growing numbers of workers required at the munitions factories at Woolwich Arsenal.

Men's hostels on Archery Road, close to Well Hall Road in around 1918. These temporary hostels were near the railway line at Well Hall.

Hostels on Well Hall Road in around 1917. The hostels stopped being used at the end of the First World War, and slowly the workers moved away. The majority of areas occupied by these hostels was taken up by new permanent housing in the 1920s.

Rose Cottage (now demolished) was located in Sherard Road close to the junction with Lassa Road.

Sherard Road looking towards Well Hall Road. The houses shown were built in 1906. Well Hall railway station was to the left.

Looking towards Well Hall railway station and the goods yard (now the site of Pullman Place) from Sherard Road, previously called Well Hall Lane in around 1905. The station was opened on 1 May 1895.

Looking towards the shops of Well Hall Parade with the railway bridge crossing over Well Hall Road. Well Hall station is to the left.

A view of Well Hall from the railway station taken in the 1930s and showing the shops in Well Hall Parade, part of the Corbett Estate and the Gordon School in middle centre of the picture.

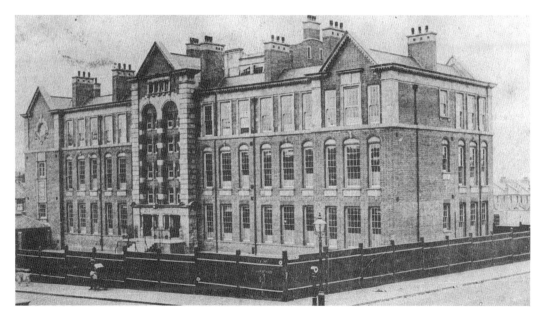

The Gordon School in 1906. The school is located on the corner of Craigton Road and Grangehill Road celebrated its centenary in 2004.

Shops on Well Hall Parade in 1903 on the corner with Dunvegan Road. It includes the Well Hall
Stores of C. Barrett, an ironmonger, and the chemist shop of the London Drug Co., as used by
Edith Nesbit and her family.

Well Hall House from Well Hall Road. The home of Edith Bland and her family from 1899 to
1922. Edith Bland is better known as the children's author, Edith Nesbit. In this house Edith wrote
one of her most famous books *The Railway Children*, which commemorates its centenary in 2005.
From her window Edith Nesbit had a view of the original Co-op store in 1906.

The rear of Well Hall House in 1904 alongside the Tudor moat. The house, built in the eighteenth century was also home to John Arnold, the famous watchmaker from 1779 to 1799.

The interior of the entrance hall at Well Hall House, taken in 1930 prior to demolition. The area around the house was purchased by Woolwich Borough Council and a park called Well Hall Pleasaunce, which opened in 1933, was created.

A plaque was unveiled in May 2004 on the site of Well Hall House to create a permanent reminder of the house and the famous people who lived there. The actor Jenny Agutter who starred in the film adaptation of *The Railway Children* officially unveiled the plaque on this most memorable occasion.

Well Hall Pleasaunce. The view was taken in the mid-1930s following the opening of the Pleasaunce and shows the pool garden looking towards the bowling green and the thatched pavilion.

The long pond, part of the Italian garden in Well Hall Pleasaunce, looking towards Well Hall Road. Following Heritage Lottery funding, the Pleasaunce has now recently been renovated and brought back to its 1930s splendour.

Above: The Tudor Barn in Well Hall Pleasaunce after restoration in 1936. The building is all that now remains of the moated manor house, which dates in parts to the middle ages. The house was home to Margaret Roper, the daughter of Sir Thomas More, Lord Chancellor to Henry VIII; her father would have visited the house when on official business at Eltham Palace. The bell shown just below the roof was retrieved from the demolished Well Hall House and was written about by Edith Nesbit.

Left: The interior of the Tudor Barn. The first floor of the building was used as an art gallery, managed by Woolwich Borough Council and their successors, the London Borough of Greenwich. The ground floor was used as a restaurant.

The rural setting of Well Hall Road in around 1903 on the road to Shooters Hill and Woolwich with Kidbrooke Lane to the left. The ancient cottages on the left are known as Nell Gwynne's Cottage.

The building to the left was known as Nell Gwynne's Cottage, a name used by Edwardian postcard publishers. The cottage was demolished in 1923 and the Shell petrol station now occupies the site. Note some of the First World War huts for munitions workers' families in the background.

Nell Gwynne's Cottage in 1907. A rear view of the cottage. It would be nice to think there was a connection with the famous lady from Charles II reign, but no evidence exists.

The Centre Path in Well Hall Road in the Well Hall Estate. With the start of the First World War came the need for extra housing for munitions workers at the Royal Arsenal in Woolwich. In February 1915 work began on building the Well Hall Garden City, known today as the Progress Estate.

Well Hall Road. The Progress Estate was built between February and December 1915. In just eleven months no fewer that 1,300 dwellings were built, and these were a mixture of houses and flats. This was an astonishing achievement at that time. It is interesting to think that the inspiration for the cottage design of these houses may have come from nearby, Nell Gwynne's Cottage.

Lovelace Green in 1918. The whole estate was reminiscent of a village atmosphere. The effect was achieved by the use of varied and traditional English building materials with the result that no two houses are alike. The green was planned as the major recreational open space for the Progress Estate and was used as allotments in the Second World War. The trees shown may have been original field boundaries.

A No.44 tram making its way up Well Hall Road towards Woolwich. The route from Eltham church to Beresford Square in Woolwich started in 1910. The tram service ended in 1952.

Another view of a No.44 tram, this time heading down Well Hall Road to its destination at Middle Park Avenue. The view is outside the shops on Eltham common at Dunblane Road. The Welcome Inn restaurant can be seen on the left at the corner with Westmount Road.

four

Eltham
Park

Eltham Park station. The station opened in 1908 and was originally known as Shooters Hill and Eltham Park station – the name changed to just Eltham Park in 1927. The photograph was taken shortly after the opening of the station in 1908 and before a row of shops numbered 1-6 Shooters Hill Parade were opened in 1910.

Eltham Park station in 1913. This is a later view than the earlier photograph, which includes the Shooters Hill Parade shops. The station closed in 1985 along with Well Hall station when the new station at Eltham was opened. Note the Corbett estates office board and the church of St Luke in the background.

Looking down to the London bound platform at Shooters Hill and Eltham Park station shortly after the station opened in 1908. Note the station sign showing Shooters Hill and Eltham Park. The station served the many commuters living on the Corbett Estate built between 1900 and 1914.

Westmount Road in 1928. Shooters Hill Parade shops are shown on the right. Cameron Corbett, a property developer, was very influential in the building of the new railway station. The housing estate named after him was a large area of some 334 acres. Corbett was a Scot and had all the roads of the estate named after Scottish places.

Shooters Hill Parade in Eltham Park in 1908. Corbett was responsible for providing these local shops for the housing estate.

Bread delivery handcart on the Corbett Estate in 1920. The baker, Frederick Cook, had two shops on Eltham High Street, one at the corner of Pound Place, opposite Eltham Library, and the other adjacent to T he White Hart public house.

The side of Park House (opposite Eltham Park Station) and Dunvegan Road in 1914. St Luke's Vicarage and the nearby shops on Westmount Road now occupy the site.

Westmount Road in around 1917 looking towards Shooters Hill. The church of St Luke can be seen on the left. Note the temporary hutments for munitions workers in and around Greenva Road.

IN MEMORY OF THE PAST.

OPENED SEPTEMBER, 1902.   CLOSED SEPTEMBER, 1905.

Eltham Park Wesleyan Methodist Church, Earlshall Road.

Eltham Park Wesleyan Methodist church in Earlshall Road. With the development of the Corbett Estate there was a great need for churches. The first church to be consecrated in 1902 was this corrugated iron building built between Earlshall Road and Elibank Road. With the increase in church numbers the building was replaced with the present day Methodist church.

The Corbett houses in Earlshall Road in around 1915. Part of the Eltham Park Wesleyan Methodist church can be seen on the right by the railings. Parts of Earlshall Road were some of the first housing to be developed on the Corbett Estate.

Above & below: These early pictures of Eltham Park Wesleyan Methodist church, which stands on the corner of Westmount Road and Earlshall Road, show it soon after it opened its doors on 25 April 1906.

A group of children probably from the church of St Luke leaving on an outing. The church was located on the corner of Westmount Road and Dumbreck Road and built in 1906. A local photographer, Edwin Langton of Greenvale Road, took the photograph.

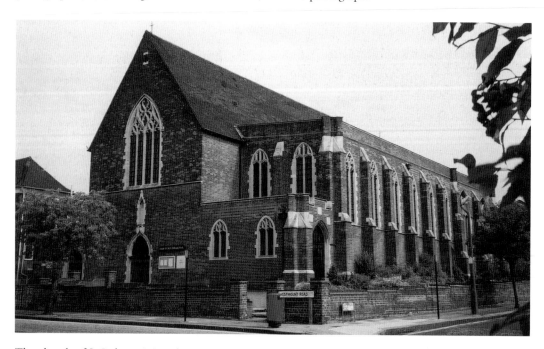

The church of St Luke as it is today.

Eltham Park in 1909. Edwardian children among a blown-down tree in Eltham Park. A newly completed house on the Corbett Estate can be seen in the background.

Eltham Park in around 1916. There were large areas of open space Eltham Park South renamed in the 1920s, London County Council acquired the area in 1903.

Park Side (now Glenesk Road) overlooked the large open space of Eltham Park.

Eltham Park recreation ground in around 1906. There had been plans to build on this land for housing for the Corbett Estate, but the London County Council intervened and the area was saved for recreational use.

Greenholm Road in 1905. Greenholm Road, located between Eltham High Street and Glenure Road, is part of the Corbett Estate. Residents of the road celebrated the centenary in 2000 with an exhibition and a book published on the history and past residents of the road.

Pippin Hall Farm around 1912. The dairy farm was located on Bexley Road near Glenesk Road and a short walk from Greenholm Road.

Park Farm Place, acquired by Sir William James in 1774. As a commander for the East India Co. he became famous during his naval campaigns off the coast of India particularly at Severndroog near Bombay attacking pirates. Following his death in 1783 Lady James erected a memorial to him for his achievements. The tower is shown in the distance at Shooters Hill and was called Severndroog Castle.

Opposite Above & below: These shops in Eltham High Street opposite Southend Crescent, known as Eltham Broadway, were built to serve the residents of the Corbett Estate. The spire type structure was constructed by Thomas Chester Haworth and called The Monument. It served as a fumigation shaft over a sewer. It was demolished in 1932.

CONVENT ST. CLOTILDE,
ELTHAM PARK.

All: Today there are few traces of Park Farm Place at Glenure Road. The mansion was demolished in 1912 after St Clotilde's convent school acquired the site and built this new building, which is seen here in approximately 1933. The school remained on the site until 1938. Today the building is used by St Mary's Roman Catholic School.

SEVENDRORG CASTLE, SHOOTERS HILL   594

Above & right: Two views of Severndroog
Castle in Castle Woods off Shooters
Hill from the early 1900s. The building,
a three-storey triangle-plan tower,
was acquired by the London County
Council in 1921 and provided a place
for refreshments and commanding views
towards central and east London. In
recent years the building has been closed
to the public and become neglected. A
preservation trust has been campaigning
to again open it to the public as a visitor
attraction and it recently appeared on the
BBC *Restoration* programme.
An antiquarian print of Severndroog

Castle from 1807. When Lady James died in 1798 the building had a number of different owners. Lord George Rancliffe, who was the son-in-law to Sir William and Lady James and survived their deaths and his wife's, had ownership of Severndroog when this print was drawn.

five

Avery Hill

The gatehouse off Bexley Road, built in 1890. It formed part of the estate belonging to Colonel John North, who made his fortune from Chile's rich nitrate deposits. On returning to England he purchased the Avery Hill estate in 1883.

The mansion from the public park in around 1916, long after Colonel's North death in 1896. The mansion was completed in 1890 and consisted of some fifty rooms. The mansion replaced an earlier house dating back to the early 1800s.

Above: An Edwardian group
standing outside the mansion,
which became a training college for
lady teachers in 1906. Note the fire
escape by the wall of ivy.

Right: The grounds were always
popular with local residents and still
are today. The River Shuttle, which
ran across the public car park, has
its main source on the west-side of
the park and makes its way towards
Bexley before entering the River
Cray.

Avery Hill Park. This large open area of some 86 acres was opened to the public in 1903. This had formerly been connected with the nearby mansion seen in the background. The building on the right had many functions including a students' common room and is today the Park Café.

An aerial view of the mansion taken in 1920 with the gatehouse in the distance. By this time the mansion was being used for some 360 students as a teacher training college for ladies in 1906. A large part of the mansion was destroyed by enemy action in 1941.

Above & below: The imposing domed structure, known today as the Winter Gardens, from photographs taken in about 1912. The Winter Gardens are now open to the public and consist of three temperature-controlled houses, each with a fine collection of trees, shrubs, flowers and palms.

Colonel North's original entrance to Avery Hill in around 1907. The entrance survived bomb damage in 1941 and is now incorporated into the buildings, which form part of the Avery Hill campus of the University of Greenwich. The new buildings were given a Civic Trust award in 1965.

A closer view of the original entrance vestibule to Colonel North's mansion in around 1911.

Students at dinner in the college in around 1910. Note the staff seated at the high table at the right side of the dining hall.

The dining hall again in around 1910 from the other end. The hall had originally been Colonel North's ballroom and picture gallery. Note the elaborate ceiling paintings, which were restored in 1993 when the University of Greenwich remodelled the dining hall as a library.

The Lounge Avery Hill College Eltham.

Above & below: Views of the students' lounge in the college in around 1909; it was used for relaxing and studying.

Above: The science block of the teacher training college in around 1917, with part of the original mansion to the left. The road in the foreground originally formed part of the Eltham to Bexley highway. Colonel North negotiated with the authorities to move the highway further north so as to give his mansion a more dignified setting. A fine brick wall divides the road from the original mansion.

Below: The college's hockey 1st XI team of 1911.

Above & below: Parts of the gardens to the west of the mansion were enjoyed by the trainee teachers.

Above: The interior of the Winter Gardens in approximately 1905 just before the house was opened as a college in 1906.

Right: This Edwardian photograph shows the abundance of plants in the Winter Gardens. Even bananas were successfully grown.

An aerial view of the hostels off Avery Hill Road, which formed part of the teacher training college. They were built between 1912 and 1916. They were each named after famous ladies, such as Mary Somerville, Elizabeth Fry, Lady Jane Grey and Charlotte Brontë. The building on its own in the front of the picture was called Southwood House.

A closer view of two of the hostels – Elizabeth Fry and Mary Somerville.

Southwood House in 1916. This late eighteenth-century house was known to have been used by Colonel North while his mansion at Avery Hill was being built. The house was bought by the London County Council in 1908 and was renamed Margaret Roper Hall.

Southwood House was used as a convalescent home by the British Red Cross for wounded soldiers during the First World War and was known as Southwood Hospital.

Keeper's Cottage in Crown Woods Lane in 1911. Known today as Crown Woods Way, the area was transformed in the 1930s with the building of the Eltham Heights housing estate. The cottage was badly damaged in the Second World War and was subsequently demolished.

Conduit Meadows in 1906. Looking towards the Holy Trinity church and vicarage in Southend Crescent in open fields to the west of Avery Hill Park. Much of this land is now taken up by sports fields and the Green Chain Walk crosses this area.

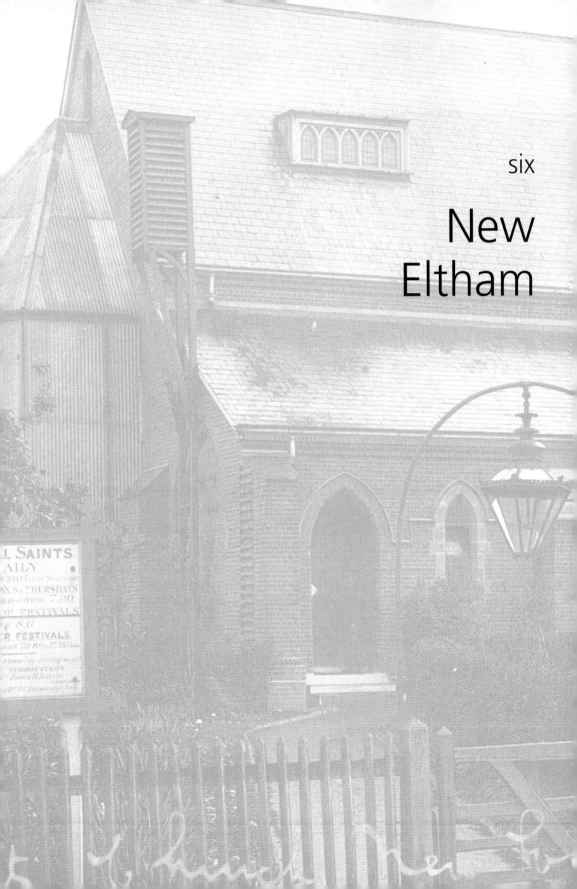

six

New
Eltham

The crossroads of Footscray Road in Avery Hill Road and Southwood Road in 1915. The development of New Eltham was a direct result of the coming of the railway and a station being built in 1878 at this crossroads, originally known as Pope Street. The station name was changed to New Eltham in 1927.

Avery Hill Road in 1932. The fenced area on the right is now the entrance to the BP petrol station.

This rural scene looks along Avery Hill Road in the early 1920s close to where it meets Halfway Street.

Southwood Road East in around 1916. The road name was changed to Avery Hill Road in 1922. The houses on the left, known as Southwood cottages, were built in the late Victorian period and still survive today.

Southwood Road in 1904. These cottages were opposite Bercta Road, which at that time was known as Southwood Road West. They were demolished in 1930 to make way for road widening.

New houses in Southwood Road looking towards Sidcup Road and the Crossways junction.

Houses in Bercta Road leading to All Saints church, built in 1898. Note the gravel and muddy state of the road.

The foundation stone of the district church of All Saints in Bercta Road was laid on the 23 June 1898. Note the temporary chancel constructed of corrugated iron sheeting supported by a timber frame on the left. With a fundraising campaign in the 1920s and '30s the church was enlarged into what it is today.

The Ace Garage was constructed in 1923 at the junction of Sidcup Road and Green Lane. Used cars are sold there today.

The public library. The library was built in 1931 in a neo-Georgian style and stands at the junction of Southwood Road and Footscray Road. The original boundary iron railings were removed during the Second World War.

This photograph of the parade in Footscray Road in 1932 looks towards The Beehive public house and Wyborne School. Some of the shops included a newsagents, bakers and drapers. Passengers will soon be alighting from the approaching No.21 bus.

The Beehive public house is on the right. It was built in 1897 and replaced an earlier inn also on this site. In this picture, the licensee is Alfred Crisp. Opposite were a row of houses called Pelham Terrace.

Footscray Road, looking towards New Eltham with Green Lane on the right before the development of housing at Cambridge Green and Clare Corner. The road was later widened and sports grounds were created on the left side of the road.

Clare Corner at the junction of Footscray Road and Green Lane. A No. 21 bus can be seen approaching the junction en route to Eltham. Note the horse trough which is still in place today. The name Clare Corner originates from the owners of Clare College in Cambridge, who also owned land in this area.

Southend Hall, New Eltham

Southend Hall in 1919. This Edwardian house was located on Footscray Road just north of
Clare Corner. The house was occupied by the military from 1937 and was demolished in 1971.
This photograph was taken before road widening took place along Footscray Road. The site of
Southend Hall is now occupied by a housing development called Inca Drive.

The Grafton factory for making office machine spools opened in 1919 at Footscray Road. When
the factory was demolished the site was taken over by the B&Q store in 1988. The factory
buildings with the fort-like frontage are shown on the right. Note the tennis courts in the centre.
Footscray Road and Southend Hall are on the left.

Footscray Road, formerly Southend Road, in 1905. This fine rural view shows Holy Trinity church in the distance on the right with what was then known as Victoria Road to the left leading to Eltham.

A closer view at the corner of Footscray Road (formerly Victoria Road) and Southend Crescent on the right. At No.59 Footscray Road, the first house past the house at the corner was the home to the writer and naturalist, Richard Jefferies, who lived there from 1884 to 1885 and is commemorated by a blue plaque. The road layout here has changed in recent times

Holy Trinity church in 1907. The church was consecrated in 1868 to serve the growing population including all of New Eltham. The church was built of Kentish ragstone by the well-known Victorian architect George Edmund Street.

A view of Holy Trinity church from Southend Crescent. The insert photograph is of Henry Arthur Hall, the church's minister from 1907 to 1942.

An interior view of Holy Trinity church looking towards the high altar. A notable feature is the Gallipoli Chapel on the south side of the chancel. The chapel is a memorial to the Gallipoli campaign of 1915-16 and was instigated by Revd Henry Hall who, as a chaplain in the British Army, was on active service in the Dardanelles. It was dedicated to him on the 25 April 1917.

A conduit head survives by a footpath to the rear of the Holy Trinity church. It fed water to Eltham Palace by means of an underground conduit, which can be sourced from what is now Eltham Warren Golf Club in Gravel Pit Lane. The view was taken about 1912 and the Green Chain Walk now passes this ancient structure. The house in the distance was known as Rusthall Lodge on Southend Crescent, which survives today and is used by the National Health Service.

seven

Mottingham

The approach to Mottingham railway station in around 1935. Note the advertisement boards on the left. The main road is Court Road, which leads to Eltham. Behind the trees on the right is The Tarn.

The Tarn in 1918. The central feature is the large lake, part of 9½ acres of woodland, lawns, flowerbeds and an abundance of birds and plants. The water from the Tarn flows into River Quaggy and then eventually into the River Thames at Deptford Creek. An interesting structure within The Tarn is the eighteenth-century ice well.

Eltham and Mottingham railway station in 1913. The station was built in 1866 as Eltham station. In 1927 the station name became just Mottingham. The station buildings partly shown on the right side still survive.

The original Royal Hotel was built following the opening of Eltham station in 1866. This photograph was taken around 1915. This is now the site of the Royal Court flats.

The junction of Court Road and Sidcup Road shows the newly rebuilt and relocated Royal Hotel of 1934. Sidcup Road was opened in 1923 and was originally known as the Eltham bypass.

This photograph, looking along Court Road towards Sidcup Road in around 1930, shows the original Royal Hotel a few years before it was demolished.

This view, looking along Court Road towards Mottingham village in around 1916, shows the Methodist church between the block of Victorian houses. It is a most rural country scene before the houses in Court Road were built in the 1930s.

The view along Court Road from Mottingham to St Andrew's church which was consecrated in 1880. This was again another rural scene before houses in Court Road were constructed. The church was aptly known as the 'church in the fields'.

The shops along Mottingham Road, *c.* 1910. Mottingham can trace its origins back to Saxon times. Also in the view is the village school where the library now stands. All these buildings survive, apart from the village school in the centre, which was replaced by the library and flats in 1968.

Another view of Mottingham Road in around 1930, looking towards the war memorial at the corner with West Park.

The war memorial and West Park. The memorial was dedicated on 26 March 1920 to those who had lost their lives in the First World War. It was designed by architect George Hubbard of West Park.

An aerial view of Eltham College off Grove Park Road. The college buildings are on the site of an eighteenth-century mansion called Fairy Hall. The Royal Naval School occupied the site from 1889 until 1910, and it is now a mixed public school.

The chapel of Eltham College at its main entrance on Grove Park Road. The foundation stone was laid on 18 July 1903 by Princess Henry of Battenburg. The chapel was dedicated on 3 June 1904 by the former Bishop of the Falkland Islands.

This view along Mottingham Road in 1916 shows the fine and imposing building of the Geffrye almshouses, which were built by the Worshipful Co. of Ironmongers in 1912. The original Geffrye almshouses in Shoreditch in London E2 are now used as the Geffrye Museum.

The Haworth Mausoleum in Beaconsfield Road in around 1905. Thomas Chester Haworth, a surveyor for Eltham and Mottingham, masterminded Eltham's first public drainage system. The first interment at this brick-built wayside structure was in 1875. Haworth was interred there in 1877.

The mausoleum was damaged beyond repair following an air raid in 1941 and the remains were re-instated below ground. The memorial stones were left on display, but the site was neglected for many years. In 2001 the gravesite was cleared of growth, the site was landscaped and a ceremony took place with descendants of the Haworth family present.

Richard Gregory and The Story of Royal Eltham

In 1909 a book was published, which even though now nearly 100 years old, is still seen today as the 'bible' for students and enthusiasts of Eltham's rich and absorbing history.

The author, Richard Gregory, was appointed headmaster of Eltham National School in Roper Street off Eltham High Street in 1901. He published a number of articles on Eltham's history in the *Eltham and District Times* before it came out in book form as *The Story of Royal Eltham* in 1909.

The book contained not only a wealth of written material on places, personalities and the history back to Roman times, but a fascinating collection of photographs showing Eltham as it was in the Edwardian period. The book contained a long list of subscribers and included Mr Hubert Bland of Well Hall, the husband of Edith Nesbit.

Mr Gregory retired from teaching in 1920 and died on 27 June 1927 aged seventy-three at his son's home in Hexham in Northumberland. His body was brought back to Eltham and was buried in a simple grave in the churchyard of St John's church.

The Eltham Society

In 2005, the Eltham Society will celebrate its fortieth anniversary. For the last forty years, the society has stood true to its aims and objectives by preserving the past; conserving the present and protecting the future. To pursue these ends the society publishes an informative quarterly newsletter containing historical topics, reminiscences from members, planning application updates and amenity issues, social events and notes on changes in the Eltham area. The society publishes a wide range of books and other material on Eltham's history, amenities, buildings and prominent citizens. Monthly lectures are held on local and other historical subjects and walks are held to remind members of Eltham's past.

Further information about the Eltham Society and the address of the membership secretary can be obtained at the information desk in Eltham library at 181 Eltham High Street. Telephone 020 8850 2268.

Eltham's town sign at Passey Place was unveiled on 11 September 1993. The sign was designed by a local architect, Paul Cookson, and paid for by The Eltham Society. It features the following historic buildings – St John's church, Avery Hill winter gardens, Eltham Palace and bridge, the Tudor Barn and Severndroog Castle. The area around the town sign was redeveloped in 2001 when improvements were made to the pavement, more seating and the addition of two trees. The area looks onto the High Street. In 1990 this area pedestrianized, which prevented traffic from entering Passey Place from the High Street.

   The building partly shown in the distance on the left is one of Eltham's oldest surviving houses, Cliefden House. This house was built in approximately 1720 and one of eight Grade II listed buildings along the High Street. The house today is used as shops and offices. The stable block associated with the house still survives in a neglected state to the rear of the house and is also a Grade II listed building.

Other local titles published by Tempus

Lewisham

JOHN COULTER AND BRIAN OLLEY

This images book looks at areas such as Blackheath, Lee, central Lewisham, Hither Green, Ladywell, Crofton Park, Catford, Bellingham, Southend Village and Grove Park. With over 200 fascinating images, never or rarely seen in print before, Coulter and Olley look at the people who made the Lewisham community what it is today. With postcards collected by those who settled in Lewisham after 1930 this book is visually absorbing, as well as being excellently written.
07524 0059 2

London: A Historical Companion

KENNETH PANTOM

This voracious city has inspired an unquenchable interest in its 2000-year history. Kenneth Panton presents the characters, events, buildings and institutions that have shaped London over the millennia, from a Roman settlement to the cosmopolitan centre of culture and commerce it is today. In an accessible, comprehensive, illustrated dictionary format, this book can be used by armchair travellers and tourists alike.
07524 2577 3

Lord's: The Cathedral of Cricket

STEPHEN GREEN

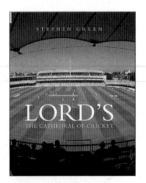

Of the many cricket venues in the world, Lord's is not only the most famous but also the one with the greatest historical importance. As the home of the MCC, Lord's is considered the headquarters of cricket. This book charts the history of the ground from its foundation by Thomas Lord in 1787 to the twenty-first century stadium. Exciting matches and great events have been a permanent feature of the ground and are brought to life in this detailed book.
07524 2167 0

British Built Aircraft Greater London

RON SMITH

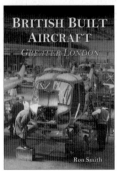

Few aircraft companies survive from the days when British aviation led the world and manufacturers such as Vickers, Avro, de Havilland, Handley Page and Sopwith were household names. From the dawn of aviation to the present day, literally hundreds of aircraft companies have closed down, gone into receivership, stopped constructing aircraft, been sold or amalgamated. Inside this book are the names and details of hundreds of firms once involved in this industry.
07524 2770 9

If you are interested in purchasing other books published by Tempus, or in case you have difficulty finding any Tempus books in your local bookshop, you can also place orders directly through our website

www.tempus-publishing.com